Screams & Whispers

Britt Alenbaugh

BookLeaf Publishing

India | USA | UK

Presentation by *BookLeaf Publishing*

Web: www.bookleafpub.com

E-mail: info@bookleafpub.com

ISBN: 9789358319538

First edition 2023

For the ones who scream for help, but their voice is only heard as a whisper.

ACKNOWLEDGEMENT

Thank you to the little girl who always had this dream. This is for you. We did it.

Bookshelves

I often stare at all the books on my shelves
I wonder about the hundreds of different stories I
have access to
I think of my story
Is it worthy enough to read
Is it even worthy enough to tell

Moon

She never really knew how to be herself
She was too invested in being what others
wanted
She never thought the real her was enough
She was scared of judgment
She was scared of letting people down
Only the moon truly knew her

Daydreaming

I find myself constantly zoning out
Daydreaming of what could've been
What should've been
Maybe that's why I have nightmares
I'm always dreaming during the day

Reflection

You're standing there
In front of the mirror
You're staring
Looking at every aspect of yourself
You keep staring
Seconds turn into minutes
Still staring
You can't even recognize the person staring back
You have no idea who your reflection is
You question who you've become

Lost & Found

5

There are two versions of myself
The person I was before she died
and
The person I was after
I'm lost
and
I will never be found

Wet Skies

6

I used to love the rain
But now it just makes me think that even God
gets sad

Winter

I've always loved the cold
I never found warmth in the sun

We Are Made of War

We never meant to hurt each other
I know this now
You were dynamite
I was a lit match
All it took was one explosion
And that was it

Question

9

I don't want the answer to most of the questions
I have
But still
All I do is turn those wheels in my head all day
I don't want the answers
But I have so many questions

A Work in Progress

I don't know how to be who you want me to
But only because
I don't even know who I want myself to be
But I do know that I don't want to be either of
those people

Enchanted

I thought it was a fairytale
When I was a little girl at least
Everything was so dreamy
That's what the movies made it seem to be
Life was always presented to be so grand and
whimsical
I thought it was a fairytale
But then life became reality
Nothing about it was an enchanting as it all
seemed
It was no longer the grand or whimsical place I
once saw
Reality slapped me in the face
The world was no longer a safe place
I thought it was a fairytale
But it was all just a joke
I thought it was a fairytale
But my reality ended up being a story that was
better off untold

Grieving the Living

You never know real hurt
Until you grieve someone
Who's still alive

For Richie

We were just kids
I didn't know that those memories would be all I
had left of you
If I knew
I would've made more
I wish I could've been the one who saved you
But as it turns out
You are the one who saved me

No Air

She was there as I took my first few breaths
I was there when she took her last
As I held her hand and watched her
I prayed that the air in my lungs would vanish
too
I couldn't breathe but I was still here
She was my air

Astronomy

15

When most people look up they see galaxies
A whole infinite of things
Yet
When I look up, all I see is you

Picture Frame

Picture perfect
That's something we never were or ever could be
But that didn't matter to us
We fought
Who got on each others nerves
We even disliked each other at times
But we were still us
We still had each other
It didn't matter where life took us
We still had us
My family was in the picture frame
The 7 of us
We will always have us
We'll always have our picture frame

Nephews

My whole heart lay in those little hands
Those boys are my reason
Without them, I wouldn't be here
They hold my heart because they are my life

Remembering Who She Used To Be

She was such a sad girl
Depression had gotten the best of her
No will to live
All of her being was dedicated to being sad
I remember that girl and my heart aches for her
She was full of so much brokenness
That girl did die
But not in a way she thought she would
She is now full of life and hope
She seeks the good in things instead of the bad
All of her being is now dedicated to saving
others
She has become the person she needed and no
one else was for her
She remembers who she used to be and that is
now her strength

The Perks of Being a Writer

19

Your thoughts finally have words

I'm Still Here

I may come and go
Sometimes I'm gone longer than usual
My brain still owns me
But I'm still here fighting
I won't lose this fight

Screams & Whispers

I felt like I was constantly screaming for help
But it was all in my head
I never voiced how I truly felt
I always thought it would only be heard as a
whisper
This is me screaming
But you'll only hear the whispers